# *Michael Collins*

# A LIFE IN PICTURES

# *Michael Collins*

# A LIFE IN PICTURES

## CHRISSY OSBORNE

MERCIER PRESS
IRISH PUBLISHER – IRISH STORY

Mercier Press
Cork
www.mercierpress.ie

Trade enquiries to CMD BookSource,
55a Spruce Avenue, Stillorgan Industrial Park, Blackrock, Dublin

Originally published by Mercier Press in hardback, 2007
This paperback edition published in 2010

ISBN: 978 1 85635 718 0

10 9 8 7 6 5 4 3 2 1

*In memory of my mother and father
and their love for Ireland*

Printed and bound in the EU.

# Contents

# Introduction

Since the publication of my first book, *Michael Collins Himself,* I have been asked to give illustrated lectures for various historical societies, both in Dublin and around Ireland, on what was to be my original book on Michael, *In the Footsteps of Michael Collins.* After each lecture I am always asked how soon will this book be available on the bookshelves, to which my reply is 'I've not started it yet!'

Now, four years after the publication of my first book, with encouragement from both Mercier, my publishers, my husband and members of Michael Collins' family (on both his father's and mother's side), as well as my many friends here in Ireland, I decided to undertake the rather daunting task of writing and producing a follow up.

This book comprises photographs taken by myself and friends, with captions illustrating some of the many locations and buildings he would have known but as they are today. It also includes rare archive photographs of both his family and people he knew, other archive material, personal items such as his Waterman's fountain pen and the GAA medal he won for sprinting in 1914.

The book follows Michael's life from his birth in West Cork in 1890 to his death thirty-one years later also in West Cork. It takes us to England, where from 1906 Michael was to spend ten years living and working in London before returning to Dublin in early 1916. After the Easter Rising, he went back to England but this time as a prisoner, first to Stafford Jail, and then two months later he was transferred, with 1,800 others, to a prisoner of war camp known as Frongoch in North Wales. After his release, just before Christmas 1916, we find him back in Dublin organising the Volunteers and building up a network of spies and informers.

Shortly after the overwhelming victory of Sinn Féin during the 1918 election and the establishment of Dáil Éireann in January 1919, the War of Independence began. This lasted two and half years until a truce was called between Britain and Ireland in July 1921. Later the same year, as one of the leaders of the delegation that met the British Prime Minister Lloyd George in London to discuss a peace treaty between the two nations, Michael was one of the signatories of the Treaty that was to give Ireland Dominion status and the right to be known as the Irish Free State. After some months of renewed bitterness between the pro- and anti-Treaty sides, civil war broke out in late June 1922 with the bombing of the Four Courts. Two months later Michael tragically became one of its victims, dying on a lonely roadside in West Cork at the age of thirty-one.

This book not only shows some of the many safe-houses and offices around Dublin that Michael and his men used during those times but also their interiors, the trap doors and secret rooms still there after eighty-seven years. During the last ten years whilst I have been researching for this and my previous book, I visited many museums, libraries, archives, military barracks, as well as people whose families would have known Michael and worked with him. They all kindly donated or allowed me to photograph various pieces of memorabilia or old photographs which bring to life how things were during those tumultuous times in Ireland at the beginning of the twentieth century.

I also touch on Michael's love life, especially his relationship with Kitty Kiernan, the Longford woman he had hoped to marry had fate not been against them. The watch he gave her when they become 'unofficially' engaged the weekend before Michael left for the Treaty talks in London is now held at the Longford Archives and Library. Unfortunately the beautiful diamond engagement ring he presented her with in March 1921, costing the princely sum of sixty pounds was lost many years ago. A copy of one of the letters written to Kitty gives a wonderful insight into Michael's state of mind during the early months of 1922 after the signing of the Treaty. Also the exteriors and interiors of both the London homes of two ladies associated with Michael in his early days, Hazel Lavery and Moya Llewelyn Davies, are featured in the book.

Sadly, some of the buildings in this book are no longer standing or have been modernised and changed beyond recognition. Even the old lime trees, that stood for over a hundred years in front of the Gresham Hotel, surviving rebellions, civil wars and emergencies, were chopped down in early 2005, to make way for the modernisation of O'Connell Street.

I hope you find this book enjoyable and interesting and should like to end this by saying I doubt if anyone other than Michael Collins himself has visited, or had access to so many places connected with his personal life other than myself and if there is anyone out there I would certainly like to meet them.

*Chrissy Osborne*

# Childhood 1890–1906

It was in the remote and beautiful countryside of West Cork, that Michael James Collins, the youngest son of farmer Michael and his wife Marianne, was born in the early hours of Thursday 16 October 1890. He was to be the last of eight children, three boys and five girls, born in a small farmhouse known as Woodfield, which had been in the Collins' family for seven generations.

Michael's mother Marianne was a local girl from just down the road at Sam's Cross and had married Michael senior on 26 February 1876 at the nearby parish church in Rosscarbery, some four miles from Woodfield. Michael had recently celebrated his sixtieth birthday, while Marianne was just twenty-three. All of their eight children were to be christened at Rosscarbery and it was here that the family attended mass each Sunday until a new church was built at Lisavaird in the late 1890s, which was much closer to Woodfield.

Lisavaird, a small hamlet just a couple of miles south of Woodfield, was where Michael first attended the local national school a few weeks before his fifth birthday. In September 1903, a month before his thirteenth birthday, he went on to study for the British Civil Service Commission's Exams for Temporary Boy Clerks at the Male National School in Clonakilty. During the week, he lodged with his older sister Margaret O'Driscoll and her family in the town square, and later in 1906 at a farm in Clogheen, a townland a mile south of Clonakilty. Having passed his exams in the spring of 1906, Michael left West Cork forever, except for annual holidays, and joined his sister Hannie in London where she was already working for the British Post Office in West Kensington.

Woodfield, the birthplace of Michael Collins, on Thursday 16 October 1890.

The interior of the original farmhouse where Michael was born.

Michael aged about eleven, with his sister Mary, grandmother, mother and brother Patrick outside the 'new house', 1901. After the death of her husband in 1897, Marianne, with the help of neighbours and a local stonemason, had a new house built and the family moved in for Christmas 1900.

Photo, said to be of
Michael's Uncle Patrick,
taken around 1880.

The 'Old Burnt House' as it was later known locally.
Photo taken shortly after Woodfield was torched by the
Essex Regiment in April 1921.

Another photo of the family group outside the 'new house'. Right to left: brother Johnny, unidentified but possibly a neighbour, sister Mary, mother Marianne, sister Katie, maternal grandmother Johanna O'Brien and sister Margaret. Young Michael can just be seen on the far right of the group.

ST FACHTNA'S PARISH CHURCH, ROSSCARBERY, WEST CORK

St Fachtna's parish church, Rosscarbery - exterior and interior. It was here that Michael's parents were married on 26 February 1876 and all their eight children christened. Although a four-mile journey from Woodfield, the family attended mass here until a new church was built in Lisavaird.

SAM'S CROSS, NEAR CLONAKILTY, WEST CORK
The O'Brien farm at Sam's Cross. The house built in 1910 was a replica of the
Collins' house in Woodfield. Adjacent to it is the original farmhouse where
Marianne, Michael's mother, together with her brothers and sisters, were all born.

CHURCH OF THE SACRED HEART, LISAVAIRD, WEST CORK
After this church was built in the late 1890s, Michael's family came here to
mass as Lisavaird was much closer to Woodfield than Rosscarbery. It was here
that Michael, along with his cousin Jim O'Brien, were altar boys.

THE OLD NATIONAL SCHOOL AT LISAVAIRD, WEST CORK

A few weeks before his fifth birthday in October 1895, Michael began attending Lisavaird National School, where he remained a pupil until 1903. Its headmaster Denis Lyons, a member of the IRB (Irish Republican Brotherhood, an organisation set up to overthrow British rule in Ireland), was to have a great influence on young Michael, as was James Santry, an old Fenian, who was the blacksmith in the village.

MICHAEL'S CHILDHOOD AROUND WOODFIELD

'Knockfeen', the large hill across from Woodfield with breathtaking views across Co. Cork and Kerry, which Michael and his family would occasionally climb, as he did for the last time with his brother Johnny on Christmas Day 1921.

ABOVE: Longstrand, one of the beaches closest to Woodfield. During the summer Michael, taking the reins, would drive his mother and sisters here by pony and trap, where they would picnic and bathe, although he himself never learned to swim.

BELOW: The small stream that flows through the valley below Woodfield. Young Michael fished and played along its banks with his family and friends.

CLONAKILTY

The Male National School, Clonakilty, West Cork. Michael attended this school from October 1903 until February 1906 to study for the British Civil Service Commission's Exams for Temporary Boy Clerks. Going to Cork city in February 1906, he sat the exam in University College Cork. Having obtained excellent results, he left West Cork to join his sister Hannie in London (she was already working for the post office as a clerk).

BELOW: Inkstand from the desk used by Michael later in life as Minister for Finance.

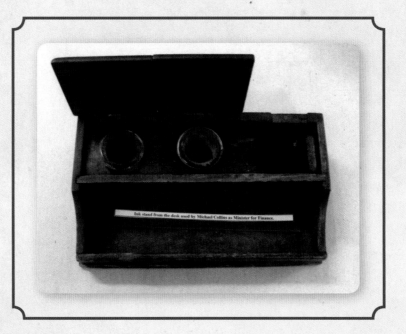

No. 6 Emmet Square, Clonakilty where Michael first went to live during the week with his sister Margaret and family, whilst attending the local National School, only a two minute walk away.

Clogheen, a townland just outside of Clonakilty. Michael's sister Margaret and her husband Patrick along with their family, moved to this farm in early 1906. Michael also stayed with them here during the week in the early part of 1906. He was by then the proud owner of a bicycle and cycled to school each day.

This jacket was made for the fifteen-year-old Michael by 'Santry's Tailors' of Clarke Street, Clonakilty for his journey to London.

The old station, Clonakilty. It was from here in July 1906 that Michael caught the local train to Cork city. From there he boarded the Cork Steam Packet that took him around the south coast of Ireland, past the tip of Wales and then along the southern coastal counties of England before eventually entering the Thames estuary and into the city of London. Disembarking at Whitechapel in London's East End, Michael was met by his sister Hannie and the second phase of his life was about to unfold.

# Early days in London

In July 1906 Michael Collins, three months short of his sixteenth birthday, disembarked from the steamer that had taken him from Cork harbour to the docks at Whitechapel in London's East End. He spent the next ten years living and working in London. During that time he lived at four different addresses with his sister Hannie and his career progressed from working as a boy clerk for the Post Office Savings Bank in Hammersmith to working in the City for three different financial institutions. From them he gained the knowledge and experience he would need on his return to Ireland in 1916 in his role as secretary for the National Aid Fund, and later as Minister for Finance in the First Dáil.

Hannie introduced Michael to London theatres and art galleries, and to the London Irish Society, where he was to meet Moya Llewelyn Davies, known to him through his membership of the Gaelic League, and her husband Crompton. Later, he also became friends with Hazel and Sir John Lavery and through these prestigious contacts, Michael mixed in the upper-class world of London, gaining an understanding of the English ruling-class psyche, which was to stay with him for the rest of his life.

He also had a great interest in the Gaelic Athletic Association (GAA) and in 1910 became secretary for the local Geraldines Hurling Club, as well as playing for them. He also enjoyed athletics and was particularly good at sprinting and the long jump.

Michael's interest in Irish independence resurfaced early in his career at the Post Office. In 1907, he joined the London branch of Sinn Féin and Sam Maguire, a fellow worker, enrolled Michael into the Irish Republican Brotherhood (IRB) in 1909. By 1914, he was promoted to treasurer for the London and South-Eastern District of the IRB and in April 1914, along with his cousin Seán Hurley, enlisted with London Brigade of the Irish Volunteers.

6 MINFORD GARDENS,
SHEPHERDS BUSH

In July 1906, Michael joined his
sister Hannie at her small bed-
sit in Shepherds Bush,
West London.

Hannie, seen here in
later life.

Two handkerchiefs given to Hannie by Michael.

POST OFFICE SAVINGS BANK, BLYTHE ROAD, HAMMERSMITH
It was here that Hannie had been working as a clerk some years before her
young brother joined her in July 1906 as a boy clerk. Their flat in Minford
Gardens was just a ten-minute walk away.

11 COLEHERNE TERRACE,
CHELSEA
In 1908, Hannie and Michael
decided to move to a larger
flat - in what is now known
as Brompton Road. Their
flat was above a bakery.


CARNEGIE LIBRARY,
SHEPHERDS BUSH ROAD
Just around the corner from
Minford Road was the newly
opened library where, under
his sister's influence,
Michael spent many hours.

KING'S COLLEGE, THE STRAND

Also in 1908, Michael studied here for the post of assistant clerk in the British Civil Service. He passed the exam successfully in 1910. He also had to undertake a medical examination which found him physically fit but in need of dental treatment. Michael had a fear of dentists and at this point decided against a career in the civil service.

HORNE & COMPANY, STOCKBROKERS, MOORGATE STREET

No. 23, now gone, was where the offices of Horne & Company, Stockbrokers stood. Michael left the Post Office Savings Bank in April 1910 and went to work here as a clerk in charge of the messengers.

28 PRINCES ROAD, NOTTING HILL

This small artisan house was to become Hannie's and Michael's third home from 1913 to 1914. Michael had a great empathy with the Notting Hill area, one of his favourite books being "The Napoleon of Notting Hill" by G.K. Chesterton.

Princes Road was also within walking distance of the Coronet Theatre, the London venue for the Manchester Repertory Company, of which Michael was a great supporter. Moya Llewelyn Davies and her husband Crompton, good friends of Hannie and Michael, lived quite close by in Camden Hill Gardens. Occasionally they would spend an evening together at the Coronet or sometimes the Court Theatre, now the Royal Court, in Sloane Square.

LEFT: The Coronet Theatre, Notting Hill Gate.

Court Theatre, Sloane Square, Chelsea.

1 Camden Hill Gardens, Holland Park, home of the Llewelyn Davies from 1910.

Moya Llewelyn Davies with her young son, Richard, 1913.

Crompton Llewelyn Davies with his daughter, Catherine, 1915.

BOARD OF TRADE, WHITEHALL
Michael worked here as a clerk from September 1914 until May 1915,
in what was then known as the Labour Exchange.

5 NETHERWOOD ROAD,
WEST KENSINGTON
This was Michael's final
London home before
returning to Ireland in
January 1916. He, along with
his sister, had moved to
this address in 1914. Hannie
continued living here until
the 1940s when she retired
and returned to Ireland.
It was a spacious flat
above a dairy, comprising
two bedrooms, sitting-room,
kitchen and bathroom, which
in 1914, was considered a
luxury.

MORGAN GUARANTEE TRUST OF NEW YORK, LOMBARD STREET
From May 1914 until January 1916, Michael worked for this American bank as a clerk. His main reason for joining the company was the possibility of getting a transfer to America if conscription came in and he was forced to join the British army.

His older brother Patrick had gone to live in America some years before and was a member of the Chicago police force. He had mentioned to Michael in his letters that he was welcome to join him and his family in Chicago, where there was plenty of work to be found.

Patrick shortly after his arrival in America in the early 1900s.

Patrick in later life as captain in the Chicago police.

THE GAELIC ATHLETIC ASSOCIATION IN LONDON

ABOVE: The Geraldines GAA Hurling Club with Michael, middle row, centre in dark jersey. Michael joined the Geraldines in 1908, usually playing mid field or back. By 1909 he was elected to the London County Board of the GAA and in 1910 became their secretary, a post he was to hold until 1916. He was also a member of the GAA London football team, playing alongside fellow West Corkman, Sam Maguire, who was captain of the Hibernian footballers. Michael also excelled in sprinting and the long jump.

ABOVE: The Geraldines GAA Hurling Club with Michael, middle row, extreme
left with shamrock on his jersey.
BELOW: Perivale Playing Fields, West Ealing, off the Great West Road.
Michael organised hurling matches here between 1910 and 1914.

Both sides of the medal awarded to Michael for winning the London GAA 440 yards sprint. He wore this medal on his watch chain in later life.

A page from Michael's day book for the Geraldines for the year 1910.

36

INVOLVEMENT WITH THE IRB AND SINN FÉIN
A photo of Sam Maguire, centre holding the ball, seated with his two
brothers, Dick and Bill, on his left. Taken in London 1910.

ABOVE LEFT: Barnsbury Hall, Islington. HQ of the London IRB, where Sam Maguire swore Michael into the IRB in November 1909.

ABOVE RIGHT: 115 Chancery Lane, London. In 1910, it was 'The Workmen's Legal Friendly Society' as well as a branch of the Gaelic League, known as the National Club. It was also Sinn Féin's London HQ and frequented by both Michael and his associates between 1906 and 1916.

BELOW: The German Gymnasium, Kings Cross, was used by the London Volunteers for drilling and training in preparation for the forthcoming rising in Ireland in 1916.

# Dublin, The Rising and its aftermath 1916

In early 1916, Michael returned to Dublin, lodging briefly with an aunt and her family in Inchicore, then a small village outside of Dublin, before securing a room at No. 16 Rathdown Road, off North Circular Road, and within walking distance of the city centre. Although working part time as a financial advisor to Count Plunkett, he was also employed by Craig Gardner and Company, a firm of accountants in Dame Street.

Michael was actively involved with the Volunteers and spent most of his spare time at Larkfield, the Plunkett residence in Kimmage, drilling and making bombs for the planned rising later that year.

The Easter Rising took place on Monday 24 April and found Michael, as aide-de-camp to Joseph Plunkett, resplendent in his staff-captain's uniform, assembled outside Liberty Hall, before marching the short distance to the GPO, where he was based along with Pearse, Connolly and Clarke. After several days of heavy bombardment by the British, the Volunteers, led by Michael, tunnelled their way out of the burning building and made their escape down into Moore Street spending their last night in No. 16. On Saturday 29 April, Pearse surrendered to the British and the Volunteers were then rounded up and marched along Sackville Street (now O'Connell Street) to the Rotunda Hospital, where they were held overnight in the grounds.

The following morning after the DMP detectives (G-men) had taken out the ringleaders, Michael and his companions were taken to Richmond Barracks in Inchicore and herded into the gymnasium. Further arrests were made. Michael, fortunately, was not one of these. With 238 other prisoners, he was marched down to the docks where they were put aboard a cattle boat bound for Holyhead, North Wales. From there, they were held in various prisons around England. Michael, with a few of his old colleagues, was detained in Stafford Jail for several weeks before he, along with 1,800 other Irishmen, was transferred to a former German prisoner of war camp, Frongoch, in North Wales. Just before Christmas 1916, Michael, along with 600 other men, was released and taken by train to Holyhead where they were put aboard a steam packet bound for Dublin.

16 RATHDOWN ROAD, DUBLIN
ABOVE LEFT: The exterior of Michael's residence in Dublin - the home of Mrs Sarah
Lee and family at the time of the Easter Rising. ABOVE RIGHT: The interior of No. 16,
entrance hall and stairs leading to Michael's room at the top of the landing.

CRAIG GARDNER & CO., 41 DAME STREET, DUBLIN
The exterior of the stone four-storey building on the corner of Dame Street and Trinity
Street where Michael worked part-time for Craig Gardner, from January to April 1916.
Gardner's offices were based on ground floor which has changed little since Michael's time.

GENERAL POST OFFICE, O'CONNELL STREET, DUBLIN

The GPO on what was then known as Sackville Street, now O'Connell Street, used by the rebels as their HQ during the 1916 Rising. Michael was based mainly in the 'operations' room which was above the portico over the entrance of the building.

THE INTERIOR OF THE GPO DURING THE EASTER RISING 1916
This view of the GPO interior during Easter Week 1916 ascribed to Walter
Paget, shows the wounded James Connolly on a stretcher with Pádraig Pearse
standing to his right. A graphic illustration of the chaos and bloodshed
inside the GPO during the fighting.

# POBLACHT NA H EIREANN.

## THE PROVISIONAL GOVERNMENT
### OF THE
# IRISH REPUBLIC
## TO THE PEOPLE OF IRELAND.

IRISHMEN AND IRISHWOMEN : In the name of God and of the dead generations from which she receives her old tradition of nationhood, Ireland, through us, summons her children to her flag and strikes for her freedom.

Having organised and trained her manhood through her secret revolutionary organisation, the Irish Republican Brotherhood, and through her open military organisations, the Irish Volunteers and the Irish Citizen Army, having patiently perfected her discipline, having resolutely waited for the right moment to reveal itself, she now seizes that moment, and, supported by her exiled children in America and by gallant allies in Europe, but relying in the first on her own strength, she strikes in full confidence of victory.

We declare the right of the people of Ireland to the ownership of Ireland, and to the unfettered control of Irish destinies, to be sovereign and indefeasible. The long usurpation of that right by a foreign people and government has not extinguished the right, nor can it ever be extinguished except by the destruction of the Irish people. In every generation the Irish people have asserted their right to national freedom and sovereignty : six times during the past three hundred years they have asserted it in arms. Standing on that fundamental right and again asserting it in arms in the face of the world, we hereby proclaim the Irish Republic as a Sovereign Independent State, and we pledge our lives and the lives of our comrades-in-arms to the cause of its freedom, of its welfare, and of its exaltation among the nations.

The Irish Republic is entitled to, and hereby claims, the allegiance of every Irishman and Irishwoman. The Republic guarantees religious and civil liberty, equal rights and equal opportunities to all its citizens, and declares its resolve to pursue the happiness and prosperity of the whole nation and of all its parts, cherishing all the children of the nation equally, and oblivious of the differences carefully fostered by an alien government, which have divided a minority from the majority in the past.

Until our arms have brought the opportune moment for the establishment of a permanent National Government, representative of the whole people of Ireland and elected by the suffrages of all her men and women, the Provisional Government, hereby constituted, will administer the civil and military affairs of the Republic in trust for the people.

We place the cause of the Irish Republic under the protection of the Most High God, Whose blessing we invoke upon our arms, and we pray that no one who serves that cause will dishonour it by cowardice, inhumanity, or rapine. In this supreme hour the Irish nation must, by its valour and discipline and by the readiness of its children to sacrifice themselves for the common good, prove itself worthy of the august destiny to which it is called.

Signed on Behalf of the Provisional Government,

THOMAS J. CLARKE.
SEAN Mac DIARMADA. THOMAS MacDONAGH.
P. H. PEARSE. EAMONN CEANNT.
JAMES CONNOLLY. JOSEPH PLUNKETT.

THE 1916 PROCLAMATION
One of the original surviving Proclamations. Pádraig Pearse, standing in front of the GPO on the afternoon of Monday 24 April 1916, read this out to the astounded and bemused passers-by.

MICHAEL AS STAFF CAPTAIN

Twenty-five-year-old Michael was staff captain and aide-de-camp to Joseph
Mary Plunkett, one of the leaders and signatories of the Proclamation.
This photo shows Michael wearing his Volunteer's uniform; the one he wore
when he gave the oration over Thomas Ashe's grave at Glasnevin Cemetery in
September 1917. However, it is unlikely to be the uniform he wore during the
Rising, as this was badly scorched by flames in the GPO.

## GOLD POCKET WATCH

A gold pocket watch given by order of Thomas Clarke to Joseph Derham, a young Volunteer from Skerries, North County Dublin. Clarke had asked him to be the garrison timekeeper in the GPO but as Joseph did not possess a watch Clarke then gave him this watch saying it had been intercepted through the post in the GPO. Interestingly, however, the initials on the back of the watch are M.J.C. - Michael John Collins? Michael happened to be in the same garrison as Clarke and Joseph Derham.

## JOSEPH DERHAM'S 1916 AND WAR OF INDEPENDENCE MEDALS

After the Rising, Joseph was rounded up with the rest of the rebels and sent to Wandsworth prison in England and later joined Michael in Frongoch Camp in North Wales. During the War of Independence, he was captain of the local Skerries IRA Volunteers. Later in 1922 Joseph, although he was neutral during the Civil War, met Michael for the last time in the Imperial Hotel in Cork, the night before he left for Béal na mBláth.

## 16 MOORE STREET, DUBLIN

In 1916, this was a fishmonger's shop and was taken over by the rebels after they had fled from the blazing GPO. Michael led the small party of survivors, including Pearse, Tom Clarke and the wounded Connolly. Leaving the GPO, Michael with a pistol in each hand, returning the enemy's fire and shouting encouraging remarks to his men, led them across the barricade into Moore Street where they eventually tunnelled their way through the buildings as far as No. 16, where they set up their new HQ.

## THE ROTUNDA HOSPITAL

After Pearse's surrender on Saturday 29 April at 3.30 p.m., the rebels were rounded up and their arms grounded. Before being marched off to the Rotunda Hospital grounds, Michael glanced up to the smouldering ruins of the GPO and noticed that the tricolour, which his cousin Gearóid O'Sullivan had hoisted just a few days before, was still flying. The rebels were held in the hospital grounds overnight without any food, water or shelter. Early next morning they were confronted by the DMP (Dublin Metropolitan Police) detectives who arrested the leaders of the rebellion before allowing the British army to escort the remainder of the now demoralised and weary men, including Michael, across the city to Richmond Barracks, Kilmainham.

RICHMOND BARRACKS, KILMAINHAM
Exterior of the only remaining building of the barracks, now a school
and gymnasium.

The interior of the gymnasium where Michael and his comrades were
scrutinised again by the detectives and further arrests were made before
the lucky ones, including Michael, were marched down to the docks and
herded onto a cattle ship, *Slieve Bloom*, bound for Holyhead in North Wales
and then on to various prisons in England.

## STAFFORD JAIL

For the first three weeks, the rebels were segregated and confined to their cells. Then 'free association' was allowed and Michael, realising that having been 'cooped up' for so long, he and his fellow prisoners needed exercise, organised such games as Gaelic football and 'Weak Horse', a boisterous game of leap frog. Michael, now Irish Prisoner 48F, with colleagues on the balcony of Stafford Jail.

1. Joseph Sweeney 2. Thomas Gifford 3. John G. Kilgallon 4. Fintan Murphy 5. ? 6. Cunan MacGinley 7. Eamonn Bulfin 8. Desmond Ryan 9. Colm Ó Murchadha 10. Frank Burke 11. Fergus O'Kelly 12. Michael Collins 13. Denis O'Daly 14. Dr James Ryan 15. Brian Ó Seoighe 16. Dr Eamonn Dore.

ABOVE: A game of football. The body language and appearance of the man, centre with arms akimbo and notebook in back pocket, bears a striking resemblance to Michael Collins.
BELOW: A group of rebels in the prison yard enjoying 'free association'.

A group of rebels, including Michael Collins, in the prison yard shortly
before their departure to Frongoch Camp in North Wales.

Michael is almost certainly the 'in profile' figure seated,
second row from the front, far left.

FRONGOCH CAMP, NORTH WALES

Frongoch was originally a whiskey distillery before becoming a German
prisoner of war camp in 1914. In the summer of 1916, the Irish rebels
including Michael moved in and occupied the two camps North and South.
Michael was leader of Hut No. 32. Robert Roberts, a young Welshman who
worked in the camp at the time remembered Hut 32 as 'the noisiest in Camp
North, with ceaseless outbursts!'

ABOVE: The remains of Frongoch station and signal box originally built for the
distillery. It would have seen the arrival and departure of the rebels in 1916.
BELOW: The only remaining hut left on the camp site, now used by the local
Women's Institute for meetings.

Executed 1916
—

We'll shrine their sacred memories
  – bright to guide us on
Till hope has reached its haven
  – till gloom & grief have gone
Till Freemen's hands may fashion
  the name of fame on high

Of all who trod that pathway and
  showed the way to die
                              (Rooney)


        Miceal Ua Coileam
          Capt I.R.A
            Woodfield
              Clonakilty

Frongoch
 1916

Michael's contribution, a poem by Rooney, in one of the many autograph books
kept by the internees at Frongoch Camp during 1916.

BACK TO DUBLIN FOR CHRISTMAS
By Christmas Eve 1916, all the prisoners, including Michael,
were released and taken by train to Holyhead, where they boarded the
overnight steamer to Dublin.

A photograph of Michael, taken shortly after his release from Frongoch
at O'Crowley's Studio, Clonakilty, probably over the Christmas of 1916.

# Ireland and the Foundation of the Republic, 1917–1918

Michael returned to Ireland in December 1916 and, after a brief holiday in West Cork, Dublin became his home for the next six years. He found lodgings on Mountjoy Street in Dublin's inner northside and by February 1917, had become secretary to the Irish National Aid Fund, as well as taking an active part in the reorganisation of the Volunteers, the IRB and Sinn Féin.

During the Longford by-election in May he met the Kiernan family and his future fiancée Kitty, as well renewing his friendship with Harry Boland, a fellow member of the IRB. Joe O'Reilly, a fellow West Corkman from Bantry, who had served time along with Michael both in Stafford and Frongoch, was also back in Dublin, unemployed and down on his luck. Joe, after a chance meeting with Michael, started to work for him as both his secretary and messenger boy.

In October 1917 at a secret Sinn Féin convention held in the GAA grounds in Croke Park, Eamon de Valera was elected president and Michael Director of Organisation. Sinn Féin won both the 1917 by-election and the 1918 general election by a huge majority. Michael built up his intelligence network of spies and informers, and set up his various offices around Dublin city during these two years. He was also behind two underground newspapers and involved in both arms smuggling and a bomb-making factory.

**44 MOUNTJOY STREET, DUBLIN**
Known as the Munster Hotel, Michael along with fellow Republicans lodged here after his return to Dublin in January 1917. His room was directly above the front door.

**19 MOUNTJOY STREET, DUBLIN**
Susan Killeen, a former girlfriend of Michael's, returned from London to live with her uncle and his family in Mountjoy Street. Michael first met Susan in London and their relationship had developed as far as his proposal of marriage - which she declined.

**30 MOUNTJOY STREET, DUBLIN**
The home of Madeline Dicker [usually referred to as Dilly] and her family. She first met Michael in 1917 through her Republican interests and membership of Cumann na mBan and soon began helping him with his intelligence work. The pair later became romantically involved.

Dilly's piano in the front parlour at No. 30 where she used to entertain Michael during evenings they spent together at her home.

Trinkets given to Dilly by Michael which included a Kerry Blue Terrier medal, his cuff links and hairbrush.

Dilly in the back garden of No. 30, together with two of her brothers
and a baby, possibly a niece.

VAUGHANS HOTEL, PARNELL SQUARE, DUBLIN
The hotel, consisting of three Georgian terrace houses, was one of the main meeting places of the IRA and IRB, and was also used as a hotel by the Volunteers. Later, during the War of Independence, Michael was to call it his 'Joint No. 1'. From the landing window the Dominican church where he occasionally took refuge during that time, can be seen.

THE GREVILLE ARMS HOTEL, GRANARD, CO. LONGFORD

The Kiernan family, four sisters and their brother Larry, ran the Greville Arms where Michael and his friend Harry Boland were staying during the by-election of May 1917. Kitty, one of the sisters, was Harry's girlfriend although later she was to switch her affections to Michael. Another sister Maud was engaged to Thomas Ashe who was to die, because of force-feeding while on hunger strike, a few months later in September.

BELOW: Granard from The Mote - a place Michael and Kitty loved to visit on a clear day for the views across Ireland.

Michael and Harry together in the grounds of the Mansion House,
rivals in love for Kitty Kiernan.

Kitty Kiernan, taken around the time of her official engagement to Michael, March 1922.

FUNERAL OF THOMAS ASHE

Michael was to make his first public appearance at the graveside in
Glasnevin Cemetery of Thomas Ashe, a fellow Volunteer and internee of
Frongoch, who had died because of force-feeding in Mountjoy Prison on
25 September 1917. Michael, resplendent in his full Volunteer uniform, gave
a short but revealing tribute in both Irish and English: 'Nothing remains
to be said. The volley which we have just heard is the only speech which is
proper to make above the grave of a dead Fenian'.

Admittance card belonging to a cousin of Ashe's, to attend the burial at Glasnevin. As a large number of mourners were expected to be present at the funeral, invitations were sent to close family and friends.

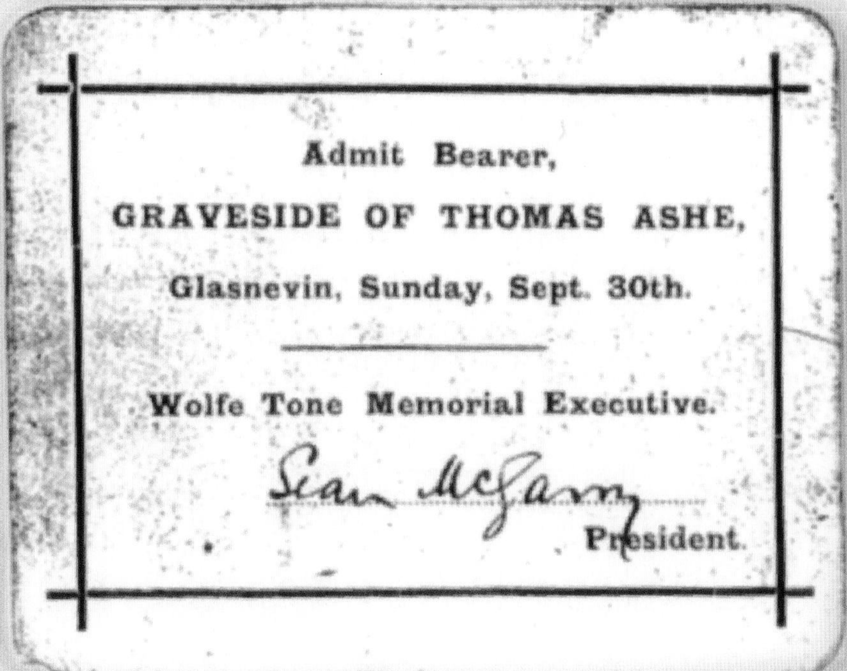

Admit Bearer,

**GRAVESIDE OF THOMAS ASHE,**

Glasnevin, Sunday, Sept. 30th.

Wolfe Tone Memorial Executive.

*Sean McGarry*

President.

32 BACHELORS WALK, DUBLIN

From early 1918, Michael used a room above what is now Toolin's Travel
as his main office, which was never raided. O'Connell Bridge, spanning the
River Liffey, can be seen from the window.

BELOW: Interior of the office used by Michael.

OGLAIŠ NA H-ÉIREANN.

Dublin
25/8/18

Dear Alderman

I have got an account from a
friend of mine in Limerick that the case of
Mícéal de Lucy is very very serious. He has been
on the run since the night of May 17th and he
has no means whatever of support as his
salary, since the refusal of the L.G.B. to sanction
his appointment, had been precarious. It is
beyond doubt that were it not for the good
offices of a few friends he would be in a hopeless
position now. His wife lives at Loughmore House
Mungret. and he has I think a few children.
He wrote me a note himself in which he makes
a bitter reference to the H Conference Fund. He says "I
am on the run now since the German Plot & the
Defence Fund never enquired if I was starving or not".
I'd take the liberty of suggesting that you should
send on £20 at once & get the full particulars
afterwards from Mrs De Lacy. Anyway take my word
for the urgent need.

Yours sincerely
Mícéal Coleáin

Letter written by him dated 25 August 1918.

SLIGO JAIL

In April 1918, Michael was
arrested outside his Bachelors
Walk office and brought to
Longford Assizes, where he was
charged for making a speech
'likely to cause disaffection
to His Majesty' at Legga, Co.
Longford. He was then taken to
Sligo Jail and held on remand
in solitary confinement for
three weeks, after which he was
released on bail.

ABOVE: The Prison Governor's
House, Sligo Jail.

RIGHT: Michael's cell in Sligo
Jail.

**13 FLEET STREET, DUBLIN**

On this site in Dublin's Temple Bar area stood the offices of The General Advertiser and Wood Printing Works Ltd, printers and publishers, where, during 1918/19, Michael became involved in the production of *The Irish World* and the Volunteers' underground newspaper *An t-Óglach*, both of which came under the trade name of The New Ireland Publishing Co. The RIC's *Constabulary Gazette* was also printed on the premises.

# AN τ-ÓᵹLÁC

## OFFICIAL ORGAN OF THE IRISH VOLUNTEERS.

VOL. II. No. 1.                              [PRICE TWOPENCE.

## THE VOLUNTEER OUTLOOK

The end of the War is not yet; nor is it in sight. The League of Nations which is talked about promises to be a sham or worse. In the future as in the past nations will win and maintain their freedom by the sword and by the threat of the sword, by war and by readiness for war. It is needful that we should fully realise this fact; for Ireland's future must be ruled by the universal law. No people can be free that is not willing to fight for freedom. The nation that strikes for its rights will sooner or later have friends and assistance. The nation for which no shots ring out and for which no steel is reddened will lie like a bone in a kennel. International complications will bring in no profit. Its enemies may rend each other, but until its own children have risen in arms it can never experience aught but a change of masters.

The Peace Conference now sitting may or may not do something for Ireland. If it does anything, then most assuredly its action will be due primarily and mainly not to the sound historical basis of our claims, nor to any logical or eloquent statement of it, nor even to international exigencies, but rather to the military demand of Easter Week and to the promise and threat implied in the Republican electoral victories of last December. In this connection it cannot be too much emphasised that if the Sinn Fein triumph in the constituencies had indicated only a raised and clarified political ideal, it would have been all sound and fury signifying nothing. It did, in fact, indicate much more. It showed that the people of Ireland, generally, endorse not only the aims but the methods of the men who raised the standard of freedom in 1916. For this reason it was an event of international import. It demonstrated that here was another people resolved that there should be no lasting peace in Europe until justice was done. The Volunteers must take care that the military promise and

threat of Ireland's declaration for Republicanism does not become a dead letter. Let it be understood that the past is done with. The present and the future count for everything. It matters not how many thousands have died for Ireland if there are no more to die. The sacrifice of Pearse and Connolly and their blood serves Ireland only so long as it is an earnest of blood that may be shed to-morrow; and if we say to ourselves that there shall be no other rising and no more bloodshed for another generation, then we are doing what we can to nullify the work of those heroic men.

The business of the Volunteers is to levy war against England on any occasion which the home or foreign situation renders opportune. If they are to do their work efficiently they must take care in all ranks to preserve and cultivate the military outlook. They must always endeavour to see the situation with a soldier's eye. They must face adverse facts candidly and sanely; but they must be true to their trust and eager to perform their military function. There are plenty of other people to concentrate on discovering how to serve Ireland by peaceful means. The Volunteers must balance them by thinking always of how they shall serve the nation under arms. They should be concerned not to find honourable ways of avoiding war, but to find favourable opportunities for fighting. An army which is not pervaded by this aggressive spirit is destined to defeat. It will be surprised and out-manœuvred. It will lose its chances. It will demonstrate in force when it ought to deliver a sudden home-thrust. Its enemy will have the initiative and he will be able to suit his convenience as to action and inaction. The spirit of the Volunteers should be that of a hound straining at the leash. So will they carry on and complete the work of the men of Easter Week. If it is patent that the rank and file wait only the wind of the word to fall-to, and that those in command will be prompt to give the

6 HARCOURT STREET, DUBLIN
This building was used as
headquarters for both Sinn
Féin and the Gaelic League.
Michael also had an office
upstairs towards the back of
the building beside the fire
escape, which was useful for a
quick escape.

Group photograph taken in the back yard of No. 6 Harcourt Street, October
1918. Back row: Seán Milroy and Robert Brennan. Second row: Diarmuid
Hegarty, Michael Nunan, Dan McCarthy, Michael Collins, Vera McDonnell,
Desmond Fitzgerald, Anna Fitzsimmons-Kelly, Brian Fagan, William Murray,
unidentified. Front row: Joe Clarke, Barney Mellows, unidentified, Sinead
Mason, unidentified, Seamus Kavanagh.

Sinead Mason, who was later to become Michael's permanent secretary, on holiday on Achill Island with friends Desmond Drummond-Fish, Siobhan Betts and Ranger, the dog. Sinead is far right. The Collins family were always very fond of Sinead and had hoped that she and Michael would eventually marry.

# The War of Independence, 1919–1921

Following Sinn Féin's huge majority vote in the general election of December 1918, a new Irish parliament, known as Dáil Éireann, was set up on the 21 January 1919 in Dublin's Mansion House. Michael was initially Minister for Home Affairs but by April of the same year, the Dáil convened again and this time he was given the position of Minister for Finance. It was from this key post, together with his various other roles, that Michael was to organise and run what was to be known as Ireland's War of Independence. It was triggered the very same day as the inaugural meeting of the Dáil, 21 January, when a party of Tipperary Volunteers led by Dan Breen and Seán Treacy, killed two RIC constables who were escorting a consignment of gelignite, an explosive the Volunteers would have needed badly.

One of the first tasks Michael undertook as Minister for Finance was the setting up of the National Loan, which eventually surpassed £250,000. The launch took place at St Enda's, Pádraig Pearse's old school and was also filmed and shown in cinemas around the country. De Valera, who had been sprung from Lincoln Jail by Michael and Harry Boland in January 1919, returned to Ireland briefly before going to America for eighteen months. He was also fund-raising for the National Loan and campaigning for the recognition of the Irish Republic.

During this period, 1919 to 1921, Michael was involved with numerous jail breaks, establishing his elite assassination unit known as 'The Squad', together with setting up various intelligence offices around Dublin and organising arms and ammunition to be smuggled to the flying columns across the country.

From early 1919 to July 1921 there was a full-scale war in Ireland, when the British sent over the Black and Tans and later the Auxiliaries to assist the RIC. This led to the burning of houses, factories and even cities, as in the destruction of Cork in 1920, in reprisals for ambushes by the various flying columns and the shooting of informers and spies by Michael and his men. However, it was the events of Bloody Sunday 21 November 1920 and later the burning of the Custom House, on the orders of De Valera in May 1921, that led to a truce between Ireland and Britain being declared on 11 July 1921.

DÁIL ÉIREANN

Following Sinn Féin's overwhelming majority vote in the December 1918 general election, the first Irish parliament, known as Dáil Éireann, was set up on 21 January 1919. The new Dáil members were photographed later in the garden of the Mansion House, and included Michael as Minister for Home Affairs. Michael was unhappy about having this photograph taken, as both the RIC and the British army could easily have identified him.

Later in December 1920, the RIC's Police Gazette *Hue and Cry* used this very photograph under 'Apprehensions Sought'.

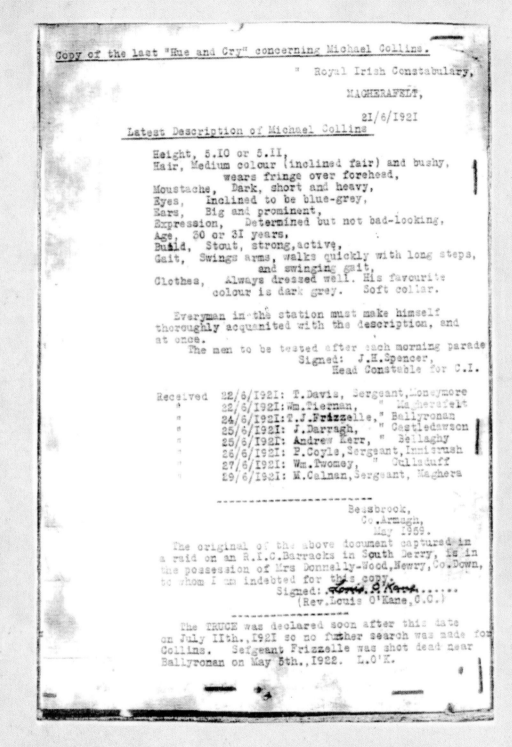

Copy of the last "Hue and Cry" concerning Michael Collins.

" Royal Irish Constabulary,

MAGHERAFELT,

21/6/1921

Latest Description of Michael Collins

Height, 5.10 or 5.11,
Hair, Medium colour (inclined fair) and bushy,
        wears fringe over forehead,
Moustache,  Dark, short and heavy,
Eyes,   Inclined to be blue-grey,
Ears,   Big and prominent,
Expression,   Determined but not bad-looking,
Age,  30 or 31 years,
Build,  Stout, strong, active,
Gait,  Swings arms, walks quickly with long steps,
        and swinging gait,
Clothes,   Always dressed well. His favourite
        colour is dark grey.   Soft collar.

Everyman in the station must make himself
thoroughly acquanited with the description, and
at once.
        The men to be tested after each morning parade
                Signed: J.H.Spencer,
                Head Constable for C.I.

Received  22/6/1921: T.Davis, Sergeant, Moneymore
    "    22/6/1921: Wm.Tiernan,   "   Magherafelt
    "    24/6/1921: T.J.Frizzelle, "  Ballyronan
    "    25/6/1921: J.Darragh,   "  Castledawson
    "    25/6/1921: Andrew Kerr,  "  Bellaghy
    "    26/6/1921: P.Coyle, Sergeant, Innisrush
    "    27/6/1921: Wm.Twomey,   "  Culladuff
    "    29/6/1921: M.Calnan, Sergeant, Maghera

                        Bessbrook,
                        Co.Armagh,
                        May 1959.
    The original of the above document captured in
a raid on an R.I.C.Barracks in South Derry, is in
the possession of Mrs Donnelly-Wood, Newry, Co.Down,
to whom I am indebted for this copy.
                Signed: Louis O'Kane
                (Rev.Louis O'Kane, C.C.)

    The TRUCE was declared soon after this date
on July 11th., 1921 so no further search was made for
Collins.  Sergeant Frizzelle was shot dead near
Ballyronan on May 5th., 1922. L.O'K.

A few months later in June 1921, in its final copy before the Truce,
the Gazette printed an amazingly accurate description of Michael,
who was still on the run.

SOLOHEADBEG

Ambush site at Soloheadbeg, Co. Tipperary. On the same day the new Dáil
was set up, 21 January 1919, a party of Volunteers led by Dan Breen, seized
a consignment of gelignite near a quarry at Soloheadbeg, which resulted in
the shooting of two RIC constables. This incident began the Irish War
of Independence. BELOW: Dan Breen on the right, together with Tom Barry
centre and Liam Deasy.

## THE NATIONAL LOAN

On 1 April 1919, the second session of the First Dáil was convened and Michael was made Minister for Finance, a position he was to hold for the next two and a half years. Under his jurisdiction, he set up the National Loan for £250,000 to fund the new government.

RIGHT: 10 Exchequer Street. Michael used a room on the top floor as one of his finance offices during this period.

BELOW: Pádraig Pearse's old school St Enda's, where the National Loan was launched.

Michael signing a bond at the steps of St Enda's.

The block upon which Robert Emmett was beheaded was used as a table for the signing of the bonds by Michael.

BELOW: A bond, dated 3 November 1919, received from Howth Sinn Féin Cumann.

Detach this part and return to subscriber.                                    No. 67/1455

**GOVERNMENT OF THE IRISH REPUBLIC.**
5 per cent. Registered Certificates (1919) (Internal).

Date, ............3 NOV 1919.................., 1919.

RECEIVED from ........Howth S.F. Cumann........ (~ B.P. Bn~)

of .......................Howth Co. Dublin...........................

the sum of ..........five.......... pounds .............................. shillings, being the amount payable on application for:—

.........a Certificate of £5..........

**MICHEAL O COILEAIN**, Minister of Finance

Per ........................

£5:0:0

Preserve this receipt carefully. It will be exchanged in due course for the definite certificate.

FULLY PAID

-3 NOV. 1919
FINANCE DEPARTMENT

GLENDALOUGH HOUSE, NEAR ANNEMOE, CO. WICKLOW
Glendalough House, the family home of Robert Barton, was used by Michael as a base for cycling around Co. Wicklow, while collecting money for the National Loan.
LEFT: The upstairs shuttered window was Michael's bedroom when he stayed with the Bartons at Glendalough House.

One of Michael's bicycles, his usual form of transport when travelling around the Wicklow countryside collecting money. The cash would be stashed away in an old leather saddlebag until his return to Dublin.

Telephone 3910.          Telegrams:—"Velocity, Dublin."

DENZILLE PLACE,

DUBLIN, June 3rd 1919

Mr. M. Collins Bachelor Walk

# SOUTHERN TAXI GARAGE,

### OPEN DAY AND NIGHT.

**PRIVATE LANDAULETTES AND TOURING CARS FOR HIRE.**

**TERMS—STRICTLY CASH.**

| June | | | £ | s | d |
|---|---|---|---|---|---|
| 1 | | To Hire of Car | £8 | 5 | 0 |
| 3 | " | | | 6 | 0 |
| | | | £8 | 11 | 0 |

Joseph A. Hanley

Department of Finance.

5th. June 1919.

... refer these papers to me
... inst. in order that I may
... eon the circumstances in
... expenditure under the two
... incurred.

Diarmuid O'Eigeartuigh

Donnchadha.

... was called up
to town on Dáil business.
The account is therefore
in order for payment
M. C.
3. 6. 19

To Secretary,
Dáil

The item for foreign affairs
is in connection with the President's
visit to the United States.

Diarmuid O'Eigeartuigh
23. 6. 1919

Please draw cheque £8.11.0

Charge as follows:—
Foreign Affairs £8.5.0.
Finance          6.0
                £8.11.0

OO'Eigeartuigh
3. 6. 18.

Daithi O'Donnchadha

A taxi bill dated 3 June 1919, shared between Foreign Affairs and the
Department of Finance.

GREAT BRUNSWICK STREET POLICE BARRACKS

'G' Division, the DMP's intelligence section, had their headquarters at this police station in Great Brunswick Street, now Pearse Street. Ned Broy who was 'G' Division's confidential clerk, had, after 1916, switched his allegiance to Michael and the cause of Irish freedom. One evening in April 1919, he smuggled Michael and Seán Nunan into the record room to spend the night searching through the secret police files there. Ned Broy, who later became a member of the Standing Committee of the Irish Amateur Handball Association, is front row, third right along, with Eoin O'Duffy, front row, first right.

1 BRENDAN ROAD, DONNYBROOK, DUBLIN
No. 1 Brendan Road was the home of Batt O'Connor and his family, one of
Michael's closest friends and was used frequently as a safe house.

One of the many keys belonging to a 'safe house' used by Michael
during the War of Independence.

CULLENSWOOD HOUSE,
RATHMINES, DUBLIN

This was originally
Pádraig Pearse's
girl's school, St Ita's.
Michael's fiancée, Kitty
Kiernan, was one of its
pupils and later 'Head
Girl'. During the period
1919 to 1921, Michael
used a room in the
basement and later a
shed in the garden as
offices.

LEFT: Kathleen (Kitty)
Kiernan, as school
captain at St Ita's.

CAPEL STREET LIBRARY
Exterior and interior of Capel Street Library (now Belle Chemine). The library was used, with the help of its head librarian Thomas Gay, by Michael and his men to pass on messages and information, which often took the form of notes left in books.

Thomas Gay's home, No. 8 Haddon Road, Clontarf. Michael met his double agents, including Ned Broy and David Neligan, both 'G' men, at Thomas' family home in Clontarf.

## THE SQUAD'S HEADQUARTERS

Michael's 'Squad', later to be known as 'The Twelve Apostles', were all members of the Dublin Brigade. It was set up in September 1919 under the command of Dick McKee, one of Michael's closest friends. They acted as soldiers obeying orders to shoot and kill spies and informers.

The Squad's headquarters was known as 'The Dump', a small room on the top floor of this building at the corner of Middle Abbey Street and O'Connell Street. The building was known as Mansfield Chambers, with Mansfield's, now Clarks, shoe shop on the ground floor.

BELOW: Some of Michael's 'Apostles'. Left to right: Michael McDonnell, Tim Keogh, Vinnie Byrne, Paddy Daly and Jim Slattery.

5 CAVENDISH ROW, DUBLIN
From a room on the top floor
of this building, now the TEEU,
Michael along with Liam Tobin,
his Chief of Intelligence,
directed their undercover
operations.

Passage in the basement of
No. 5 Cavendish Row, which
ran under Parnell Square to
Vaughan's Hotel, Michael's 'Joint
No. 1'. Seán T. O'Kelly, chairman
of the First Dáil, was also
an electrician and through
him, Michael arranged to have
electric lighting installed in
the passage.

THE MUNSTER & LEINSTER BANK
Exterior of the Munster & Leinster Bank (now the AIB) on the corner of Dame
Street and Palace Street, just beside the main entrance to Dublin Castle.

A cheque for £10,000 dated 26 July 1920, countersigned by Michael
and issued by the Munster & Leinster Bank, where he had an account.

THE STAG'S HEAD
This public house, situated just a minute's walk from Dublin Castle in Dame Lane, was frequently used by Michael to meet 'friendly staff' from the Castle.

This laneway, linking Dame Lane and Dame Street, was used by Michael to reach another of his intelligence offices across the road at No. 3 Crowe Street. His office was on the second floor of J.F. Fowler, Printers. Liam Tobin, Chief of Intelligence, also had an office here.

A view of Crow Street taken in the 1920s.

MARY COLLINS POWELL

Mary, a sister of Michael, seen here with her husband Patrick, sister-in-law and four of her nine children, lived in the Sunday's Well area of Cork city. She was very active in helping her younger brother during the War of Independence.

KATIE COLLINS-SHERIDAN

Katie Collins was Michael's closest sister, being just three years older than him. She became a schoolteacher and later married Joe Sheridan a farmer from Bohola, Co. Mayo. Michael, whenever in the area, would call over to see them. He had a secret 'dug out' in the farmyard to use as a hiding place when he was on the run during the War of Independence.

CLEARY'S, AMIEN STREET
Another public house used as a meeting place by Michael, especially for colleagues down from the north and railway workers - being across from Amien Street station, now Connolly station.

RIGHT: Upstairs room above Cleary's bar, used for meetings.

GRAFTON STREET, FORMERLY THE CAIRO CAFÉ
This white double-fronted building was the Cairo Café, a well-known haunt for English spies and informers, as well as being a tea room and dance hall.

The 'Cairo Gang' were a group of British intelligence officers sent over to Dublin to hunt down Michael and his men. This photograph shows them numbered by one of Michael's men in Dublin Castle. The shooting of these agents on the morning of Sunday 21 November 1920 by Michael's 'Squad' led to reprisals that afternoon during a GAA football match at Croke Park. Groups of RIC and Black and Tans invaded the pitch and began shooting into the crowd and at the players on the field. Fourteen people, including Michael Hogan, a Tipperary player, died, and almost a hundred more were injured.

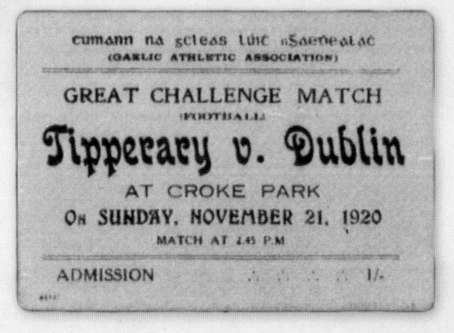

ABOVE: Bloody Sunday Match Ticket 21 November 1920.

BELOW: Michael's hand-written memorial card for two victims of Bloody Sunday, Dick McKee and Peadar Clancy. Both were tortured and then murdered by the Auxiliaries in Dublin Castle on the night of 21 November. The men had worked closely with Michael throughout the War of Independence. The card read: 'In memory of two good friends Dick and Peadar. Two of Ireland's Best Soldiers. Micheál Ó Coileáin. 25/11/20'

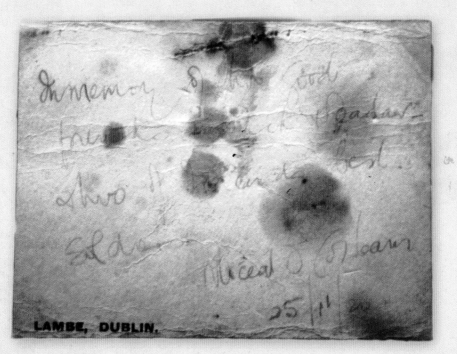

Taken at 16 Airfield Road, Dublin at the wedding of Lil Clancy and Michael O'Brien the day after Bloody Sunday, Monday 22nd 1920. Michael, seen back row second from left beside his cousin, Gearóid O'Sullivan. Both men used the house frequently as a safe house during the War of Independence.

Le ᵹac Deaᵹ-Ᵹuiᵭe i ᵹcóin

Noᵭlaᵹ Ṡonaraiᵹ,

fé meiᵭiṅ.

ó

miceál ó coileáin.

Noᵭlaiᵹ, 1920.

CHRISTMAS CARD
Personalised card in Irish for Christmas 1920.

## DESK AND CHAIR

This desk and chair was used by Michael at No. 5 Mespil Road, one of his intelligence offices which was raided by the Auxiliaries in April 1921. The drawer still bears the marks of being forced open during the raid.

AMBUSH SITES
Four locations, three in West Cork
and one in Co. Longford, used as
ambush sites by the IRA's flying
columns on the British army,
which intensified the War of
Independence.

ABOVE: Kilmichael, near Macroom,
West Cork, led by Tom Barry and
the Third West Cork Brigade on 28
November 1920.

RIGHT: Clonfin, near Ballinalee,
Co. Longford led by Seán Mac Eoin
on 2 February 1921.

Upton Station, West Cork, ambush led by Charlie Hurley on 15 February 1921.
Here the flying column attacked a stationary train carrying British
soldiers, which led to the death of three IRA men and six civilians.

Crossbarry, West Cork, again led by Tom Barry and his Third West Cork
Brigade on 21 March 1921.

THE CUSTOM HOUSE, DUBLIN

In the spring of 1921, De Valera, having returned to Ireland from America, decided to order the destruction of the Custom House, as a reprisal for 1916 and its aftermath. One of the main centres of the British tax administration in Ireland, the Custom House was an important target. With the assistance of the ASU, the second battalion of the Dublin brigade and some of Michael's 'Squad', a full-scale attack was launched on 25 May 1921.

Although the building was almost totally destroyed, the rapid arrival on the scene of the British army led to the majority of the IRA soldiers being arrested or shot. However, it was a spectacular publicity stunt for the IRA, causing chaos to the British tax system in Ireland, which had been housed in the building. Less than two months later, on 11 July 1921, a truce was declared between Britain and Ireland and led to the ending of the War of Independence.

# From Truce to Treaty, 1921–1922

Monday 11 July 1921 was the beautiful sunny day when a truce was finally declared between the British and Irish governments. There was a great feeling of euphoria throughout the country after two and a half years of war between the two nations. Within a couple of days of the Truce, De Valera as president of the Irish Republic, travelled to London and met the British Prime Minister Lloyd George, to negotiate a peace settlement. However, De Valera soon realised that the British were not going to agree to a Republic and three months later on 11 October 1921, a second delegation which included Michael, returned to Downing Street and by 6 December had successfully negotiated a Treaty under the best terms they could get.

On 7 January 1922, during a meeting of the Dáil held at the National University buildings in Earlsfort Terrace, the Treaty was ratified by sixty-four votes for and fifty-seven against, a majority of seven. The result caused De Valera and his anti-Treaty colleagues to storm out of the building. A new Provisional Free State government was set up with Arthur Griffith as President and Michael Collins as Chairman [as well as still holding his post as Minister for Finance].

From July 1921 Michael became a public figure, photographed with the Kilkenny hurling team, throwing in the ball at Croke Park, appearing at a rally in Armagh where he was the local MP. Later during the Treaty talks, he was photographed on numerous occasions both in Dublin and London, bounding out of a taxi or leaving a meeting. Around this time, he had also grown a moustache, partly as a disguise and also to appear older, as he was the youngest member of the Irish delegation that met with Lloyd George and his cabinet in Downing Street.

DÁIL ÉIREANN MEMBER'S TICKET
Ticket showing Michael as TD for both Co. Cork and Armagh,
dated 16 August 1921.

MICHAEL, WITH SEÁN Mac EOIN AND HARRY BOLAND
Michael, in contemplative mood, with Seán and Harry at the All Ireland
Final in Croke Park September 1921.

LEINSTER HURLING FINAL, CROKE PARK
Michael meets the Kilkenny and Dublin hurling teams in Croke Park,
21 September 1921.

THE MINISTER FOR FINANCE AT HIS DESK

After his return to Ireland in 1917, Michael was in many ways a deskman. His work involved a huge amount of correspondence from the setting up of the National Aid Fund in 1917, for which he was secretary, to the National Loan in 1919 and later during the War of Independence, corresponding between the various departments of Dáil Éireann, sending instructions to his flying columns and intelligence networks.

In this photograph taken around September 1921, Michael as Minister for Finance, is seated at a paper-strewn desk in one of his many Dublin offices. Michael appears to have been snapped upon hearing his name called. Quite at ease, he raises his head and turns to look at the camera. Here, a small scar on the left-hand side of his chin, the result of a childhood fall, can be seen quite distinctly.

RALLY AT ARMAGH, 4 SEPTEMBER 1921

On Sunday 4 September 1921, Michael accompanied by Harry Boland and
other close associates, travelled up to Armagh, where he was the local
Sinn Féin TD, and after a rousing reception gave a speech appealing to both
the Nationalist and the Orangemen 'to join with us, as Irishmen to come in
to the Irish nation …'

ABOVE: Michael sitting with supporters at the Armagh rally.

BELOW: ARTHUR GRIFFITH EN ROUTE TO ENGLAND
On Saturday 8 October, the Irish delegation led by Arthur Griffith,
left Dublin for London and the Treaty negotiations. He is seen here
on board the steamer bound for England, being interviewed by the press.

ABOVE: 22 HANS PLACE, LONDON. Exterior and interior showing the main staircase at No. 22 Hans Place, where the Irish delegation set up their headquarters. Michael joined them in London on Monday 10th. Talks began in Downing Street the following day and lasted nearly two months.

BELOW: 15 CADOGAN GARDENS, LONDON. Exterior and main staircase of No. 15 Cadogan Gardens, just a short distance from Hans Place. Michael took up separate quarters here, together with his close associates Liam Tobin, Ned Broy, Tom Cullen and Emmet Dalton. He also brought over his personal secretaries and two of the staff from the Gresham Hotel in Dublin.

Irish Republican Delegates Reception.
London.                                    Nov 10th 1921.

## Menu

*Soup*
Peace "thick"
Publicity "clear"

*Fish*
Hans Plaice
Caddugan Steaks

*Entrées*
Econmic Cutlets
                    (Reparation Gravy)
Minced Ulster
                    (North East Sauce)

*Joint*
Roast Beef of Old England

Aide - Memoire of Potatoes
                    (Delegates solution)

Formula of Beans
*Sweets*              (No Solution)
Compoté de Fruits Gerty, Ellie, Alice,
        *Cheese*         Kathleen, Lily.
Chaperon Duggan      Legs.
                        Minute mixture.

MENU FOR IRISH REPUBLICAN DELEGATES RECEPTION, LONDON
Interesting handwritten menu for the Irish delegation.
Note the 'compote de fruits' Gerty, Ellie, Alice, Kathleen, Lily,
all secretaries to the delegation at the time.

THE WATCH GIVEN TO KITTY

The reason for Michael's two-day delay in joining the rest of the
plenipotentiaries was that he and Kitty Kiernan were by now seriously
thinking of marriage and decided to spend the weekend together at the
Grand Hotel in Greystones, Co. Wicklow. It was the custom in those days for
couples before becoming engaged, to exchange watches. Michael's can be seen
quite clearly later in the photographs taken after the signing of the
Treaty in London. BELOW: The Grand Hotel later known as La Touche Hotel,
Greystones, Co. Wicklow.

CARICATURE OF MICHAEL COLLINS
Detail of a caricature by
an artist called Low, which
was featured in an English
newspaper, *The Star*, dated
11 October 1921, accompanied
with a caption that reads
'Mysterious Mick' Collins
(wearing his best smile
for Low).

MICHAEL IN LONDON
A preoccupied Michael,
characteristically bounding
from a taxi to one of his
numerous meetings in London.

## BROMPTON ORATORY

This famous Catholic church in the Knightsbridge area of London was where Michael attended early mass each morning, usually accompanied by Ned Broy, one of his bodyguards. After mass, he always lit a candle for his fiancée Kitty Kiernan at the altar of the Sacred Heart.

## ST MARY'S CATHOLIC CHURCH

Michael occasionally went to mass here, the church being just a couple of minutes walk from Cadogan Gardens.

## 5 CROMWELL PLACE, KENSINGTON

The home of Sir John Lavery, the painter and his American wife Hazel, who had known Michael from his early days in London. During the Treaty negotiations, the Laverys held dinner parties here in Sir John's studio, for both the Irish and British delegations. During that period, both Michael and Arthur Griffith had their portraits painted by Sir John.

MARTINSYDE TYPE A MK III BI-PLANE

This bi-plane, a Martinsyde Type A MK III, later named the Big Fella seen here in Baldonnel aerodrome, Dublin, was purchased by the Irish Provisional Government and kept on standby at Croydon aerodrome during the Treaty talks, in case they broke down and Michael had to make a rapid escape back to Ireland.

The propeller hub, the only surviving part of the plane.

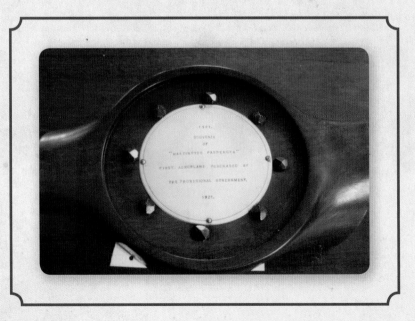

Comdt Gen. Wm J. 'Jack' McSweeny (left) and Col Comdt C.F. 'Charlie' Russell
(right) the two Irish, ex-RAF flying corp pilots who were on standby along
with the Martinsyde at Croydon aerodrome.

## THE WHITE HART (MURPHY'S) WHITECHAPEL

The White Hart, or Murphy's as it was also known, was first used by Michael and his fellow IRB colleagues during the period 1909 to 1916. Later, during the Treaty talks, Michael, now president of the Supreme Council of the IRB, again met here with fellow members to discuss the progress of the talks with the British government.

## ST ANN'S UNDERWOOD ROAD, WHITECHAPEL

It was here in 1919 at St Ann's church hall that the London Battalion of the IRA were sworn in and it was to continue as their London HQ. Between October and December 1921, Michael travelled over to Whitechapel and met with members here to discuss the progress of the Treaty talks.

OUTSIDE HANS PLACE

Some of the Irish delegation, outside Hans Place in the cold early hours of
Tuesday 6 December 1921, shortly after the signing of the Treaty. Right to
left: Liam Tobin, Michael, Arthur Griffiths, Robert Barton, Gavan Duffy and
possibly Erskine Childers.

Michael's Waterman's fountain pen, always carried in his waistcoat pocket.

months from the date hereof.

18.    This instrument shall be submitted forthwith by His
Majesty's Government for the approval of Parliament and by
the Irish signatories to a meeting summoned for the
purpose of the members elected to sit in the House of
Commons of Southern Ireland, and if approved shall be
ratified by the necessary legislation.

_Decr 6th 1921_

_On behalf of the British Delegation_

_D Lloyd George_

_Austen Chamberlain_

_Birkenhead._

_Winston S. Churchill_

_L Worthington Evans_

_Hamar Greenwood_

_Gordon Hewart_

_On behalf of the Irish Delegation_

_Art Ó Gríobhtha (Arthur Griffith)_

_Mícheál Ó Coileáin_

_Riobárd Barton_

_E S Ó Dúgáin_

_Seoirse Ghabháin Uí Dhubhthaigh_

The final page of the Treaty featuring the signatures of the British and
Irish delegations. Collins' signature is second from top on the Irish list
which is to the right. Note that he signs in the Irish as with most of his
correspondence.

MICHAEL COLLINS AND ARTHUR GRIFFITH
A weary Michael Collins and Arthur Griffith posing for the camera in
Hans Place the morning after the Treaty was signed. Michael's watch, a
recent pre-engagement present from Kitty Kiernan, is clearly seen.

CHRISTMAS IN WEST CORK
Michael spent Christmas of 1921 back home with his brother Johnny and
family who were now living with their relations at Sam's Cross in West Cork.
This photograph of Michael was taken outside the ruins of Woodfield, which
had been torched earlier that year by the British.

ABOVE: The L & N Railway Company's Hotel, North Wall Dublin, frequented by Michael and the Irish Delegates during the Treaty talks.

RIGHT: Handmade travel mirror given to Michael before embarking to London for the Treaty talks.

# The Making of the Irish Free State, 1922

Following the signing of the Treaty, Michael and the rest of the Irish delegation returned to Dublin and had prolonged and sometimes bitter Dáil debates which, except for a short break at Christmas, carried on into the new year. The Treaty was finally ratified on 7 January 1922.

On 16 January 1922, Michael as chairman of the Provisional Free State Government attended the hand-over from the British of their headquarters, Dublin Castle. The following day saw the departure of the British army, most of whom had been confined to barracks since the Truce and the ending of British Rule.

From then on Michael was constantly in the public eye, attending numerous meetings both in Dublin and London in connection with the recently signed Treaty and setting up of the new Provisional Government. He was continually being 'snapped' by newspaper cameramen and on a couple of occasions being photographed promoting new Irish products. Later that year, around the time of the election of 16 June 1922, Michael again was frequently both filmed and photographed surrounded by admirers whilst electioneering in his native West Cork.

THE MANSION HOUSE, DAWSON STREET, DUBLIN

Exterior of the Mansion House, the residence of the lord mayor of Dublin. It was in this building and the adjoining Round Room behind the Mansion House, that some of the private and public Treaty debates took place after the delegation returned to Dublin in early December 1921.

This room, known as the cabinet drawing-room, was used by members of the Dáil to discuss in private the various issues arising from the recently signed Treaty.

Michael on his way into the Mansion House to attend a meeting.

ARGUMENTS FOR THE TREATY
Michael's pamphlet on sale in early 1922.

UNIVERSITY COLLEGE, EARLSFORT TERRACE, DUBLIN

Exterior and interior of UCD Earlsfort Terrace. During December and early January 1922, further debates on the Treaty took place in a lecture room within this building. The Treaty was finally ratified by a majority of 64 for the Treaty to 57 against, a majority of 7.

Arthur Griffith on a hackney car and Michael by taxi cab, arriving
separately at Earlsfort Terrace for further discussions on the Treaty.

A despondent Michael accompanied by Joe O'Reilly, leaving Earlsfort Terrace after a long day of Treaty discussions.

My own own Kitty.                    ?5   1/1/1922

Just one or two lines.
This is the worst day I
have had yet – far far the
worst. May God help us all.
I got no letter from
you – I wonder why
In awful haste.

My, fondest love
Miceal

How did you get on
at Killashee.

A letter to Kitty Kiernan from Michael, written just before the Treaty was ratified.

DUBLIN CASTLE
It was here on the morning of Monday 16 January that the British viceroy handed over control of Dublin Castle to the Provisional Government, with Arthur Griffith as president and Michael as chairman.

Michael, together with Kevin O'Higgins, emerging from the Castle
after the hand-over formalities.

Leo Whelan's painting (below), thought to be of Michael with his newly
founded Provisional Government, is in fact his General HQ Staff, around the
time of the Truce July 1921.

CITY HALL, LORD EDWARD STREET, DUBLIN
After a brief tenure at the Gresham Hotel in O'Connell Street, the new
Provisional Government set up temporary HQ here in Dublin's City Hall.
BELOW: Michael on the steps of City Hall inspecting the first Irish National
Army troops on their way to take over Beggars Bush Barracks from the
British army, 1 February 1922. Beside him, saluting, is James O'Neill, former
commandant of the Irish Citizen Army.

Michael in Cork on St Patrick's Day, giving his opinion of the Treaty
and what he hoped he had obtained for Ireland.

RIALTAS SEALADAĊ NA HÉIREANN
(IRISH PROVISIONAL GOVERNMENT)

Reference No.

R.A.41.

BAILE ÁTHA CLIATH.

5. 4. 1922.

Mr. W. McCarthy,
48a Forest Hill Road,
Honor Oak,
E. Dulwich,
L O N D O N, S.E.22.

A Chara,

I was very glad indeed to get your letter. It was
very thoughtful of you to think of sending it.

Of course I know how easy it is for some of these
gentlemen to criticise, and how easy it is for Mr. O'Brien
to say he did not know what we were doing about the
prisoners. He knew perfectly well from the time the Treaty
was signed that I was doing my utmost in season and out of
season to secure the freedom of these prisoners. There are
some technicalities connected with some of the military
prisoners, but I have no doubt we shall secure their
release in time also. Fair criticism one does not mind,
but when people deliberately say the very opposite to what
is the truth, one cannot give them credit for the very
highest motives.

Yes, as things turned out, it was very fortunate
indeed that I had that little conversation with you. The
vote itself must show some of the leaders that their position
is not so secure as they claim when they are discussing the
present position. It may have the effect of making them
consider the rank and file a bit more. If this were done all
round, I think we might have a happier state of things al-
together.

I shall be very glad to hear from you occasionally
on how matters go generally.

Do chara,

Míċeál O Coileain

ABOVE AND ACROSS: Two signed letters from Michael on
headed notepaper also showing the title of the new
Irish government.

RIALTAS SEALADACH NA hÉIREANN
(IRISH PROVISIONAL GOVERNMENT)

MINISTRY OF FINANCE,
DUBLIN.

AIREACHT AIRGID,
BAILE ÁTHA CLIATH.

5th May 1922.

Reference No.
R.A. 195.

Mr. B. McCarthy,
4aa Forrest Hill, N.
L O N D O N.

A Chara,

      I would be glad if you could kindly let me know does attached refer to an Irish Catholic crowd?   If it does not, needless to say, I would not take any interest in the matter.

      Mise, le meas mor,

*Mícheál O Coileain*

*I hope you have been keeping well*

*M.*

The letters also show the Free State's first postage stamps, which were British stamps showing the head of King George V, printed over in Gaelic script with the words 'Rialtas Sealadach na hÉireann' (Irish Provisional Government), issued 17 February 1922.

OUTSIDE THE
PRO-CATHEDRAL, DUBLIN
Michael, together with Arthur
Griffith, Alfie Byrne and Kevin
O'Higgins having attended the
requiem mass for Pope Gregory at
Dublin's pro-cathedral on
31 January 1922.


GOVERNMENT BUILDINGS,
MERRION STREET, DUBLIN
In the spring of 1922, the
Provisional Government set up
their new permanent HQ here, in
what was originally intended to
be UCD's extension to its college
of science. Michael occasionally
climbed to the top of the dome
for views across the city.

ST FRANCIS' CHURCH, CORK CITY
Sunday 12 March 1922. Michael, having attended mass here at the church of St Francis in Cork. With him are (left to right) Diarmuid Fawsitt, Comdt Ned Cooney, Father Louise, OFM, Pádraig O'Keeffe, TD, Fathers Leo and Edmund, OFM, Comdt Seán Mac Eoin.

BELOW: Michael with a group in Killarney after a pro-Treaty rally, 22nd April 1922.

MICHAEL, THE MAN WHO WON THE WAR ON A BICYCLE

Michael, posing with the latest model of bicycle at Pearse's Factory
Wexford town, April 1922. Pearse's, a well-known company producing farming
machinery, used Michael in this advertisement as 'The man who won the war
on a bicycle', the bicycle being his main form of transport during the War
of Independence.

GROUP IN THE GROUNDS OF THE MANSION HOUSE

To try to avert a growing possibility of civil war between pro- and anti-Treaty factions, Michael and De Valera agreed on a pact for the forthcoming election on 16 June, which would allow a mix of 66 pro-Treaty and 58 anti-Treaty candidates. This photograph, taken on 20 May, shows Michael and De Valera, together with a mix of pro- and anti-Treaty candidates, in the grounds of the Mansion House.

MICHAEL ELECTIONEERING IN CO. CORK
An exhausted Michael in the back of a touring car, with Ned Cooney sitting
beside the driver. BELOW: Receiving flowers from the local children.

MICHAEL AT THE FORDSON FACTORY, CORK

Another example of Michael being used for promoting a new product, as shown in this newspaper photograph of Michael on Fordson's latest model tractor, taken in June 1922. Mr Grace, the Managing Director of Fordson's stands beside Michael, hands in pocket. BELOW: Possibly the same tractor now preserved at a steam museum near Cork city.

ABOVE: Michael addresses
an enormous crowd in Cork
city in the run up to the
elections.

RIGHT: Michael greets
supporters at a railway
platform.

THE HERO'S RETURN - ELECTIONEERING IN HIS NATIVE WEST CORK
Having been elected as TD for the area in the December 1918 election and
a member of the First Dáil in 1919, Michael spent the last few days before
the June 1922 general election back in his native West Cork, which included
his home town of Clonakilty. Here he can be seen outside O'Donovan's
Hotel, addressing an enthusiastic crowd from an open top touring car and
surrounded by friends and admirers.

THE WEDDING OF SEÁN Mac EOIN AND ALICE COONEY
The wedding of Seán Mac Eoin and Alice Cooney, Wednesday 21 June 1922.
Originally it was to be a double wedding with Michael and Kitty, but
Michael and Kitty's wedding was cancelled due to the uncertain political
situation in the country.

This sequence of photographs taken seconds apart, illustrates a high spirited Michael outside St Mel's cathedral, Longford.

Michael greets Seán Mac Eoin. The cameraman rapidly abandons his case of plates just in time for this shot. (bottom right)

Photograph of the wedding group taken outside of the Cooney home at Gurteenboy. Michael, wearing a mischievous smile, was tickling Seán's ribs and tugging the bride's veil. Later during the wedding breakfast, Michael amused himself by spraying the guests with a soda siphon.

# The Civil War, 1922

Despite the pro-Treaty party, led by Michael, winning the general election by a huge majority, the anti-Treaty side refused to submit to majority rule and continued the fight. A group of 'Irregulars' as they were known, under the command of Rory O'Connor, had already taken over the Four Courts in Dublin and set up their headquarters. It was because of this, along with the assassination of the British Field-Marshal Sir Henry Wilson in London, a long time opponent of Michael's and of Irish Nationalism, that Winston Churchill, colonial secretary with the British government, ordered Michael to bomb the Four Courts or else face the return of British troops to Ireland. This triggered the Civil War which commenced on 28 June and devastated the country over the following eleven months.

On 12 July, Michael became Commander-in-Chief of the new Irish National Army, his headquarters being Portobello Barracks, now Cathal Brugha Barracks, in Dublin. His workload changed from running the country to directing the army and endeavouring to end the Civil War. It was during Michael's tour of inspection in Munster, where some of the worst fighting was taking place, that Arthur Griffith died suddenly in Dublin on 12 August. Michael returned to Dublin to lead the funeral cortège, resplendent in his new general's uniform.

A few days later, Michael went on a second tour, this time to his native West Cork and it was here he was killed during an ambush in the evening of Tuesday 22 August 1922. He was just thirty-one years old.

### THE FOUR COURTS, DUBLIN

On 14 April 1922, a group of anti-Treaty men led by Rory O'Connor, took over the Four Courts as their HQ. By the end of June, despite the successful pro-Treaty election, they were still there. Churchill's threat to Michael to either recapture the building with his own Irish National Army or else he would send over British troops to do the job, forced Michael to order the bombardment of the building on 28 June by his own men. So began the Irish Civil War.

MICHAEL COLLINS AS COMMANDER-IN-CHIEF, JULY 1922
On 12 July, Michael became Commander-in-Chief of the new Irish National
Army and set up his headquarters at Portobello Barracks in Dublin.

Michael's living-quarters (above), his office (below) at Portobello Barracks.
where he would have lived and worked as Commander-in-Chief.

INSPECTING THE TROOPS IN NEWCASTLE WEST, LIMERICK

Michael inspecting the local Irish National Army troops in Newcastle West, during part of his southern tour in early August 1922. Most of the fighting was in Munster.

MEMORABILIA BELONGING
TO MICHAEL WHEN HE WAS
COMMANDER-IN-CHIEF

Field glasses, pouch,
Colt pistol.

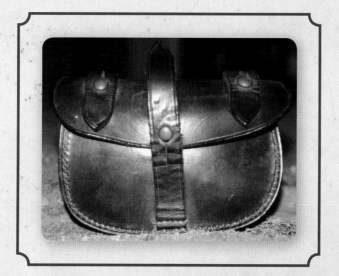

Colt Pistol
General Michael Collins
Serial No: 227003

MEETING AT THE CURRAGH ARMY CAMP
Michael as Commander-in-Chief attending a meeting at the Curragh army
camp with his fellow officers in early August 1922.
Left to right: Col Dunphy, Michael, Maj. Gen. Emmet Dalton,
Comdt Gen. P. MacMahon and Comdt Gen. D. O'Hegarty.

### FUNERAL OF ARTHUR GRIFFITH

Arthur Griffith died suddenly from a cerebral haemorrhage on 12 August 1922. Michael returned to Dublin to attend the funeral at the pro-cathedral and headed the cortège with Richard Mulcahy who was then Minister for Defence and Chief-of-Staff. Michael as a bearer, at the right hand rear of the coffin, leaving the pro-cathedral after the funeral mass.

A troubled Michael outside the pro-cathedral, waiting for the cortège to move off.

Michael heading the funeral cortège, with Richard Mulcahy, is waiting
outside the pro-cathedral for the procession to begin.

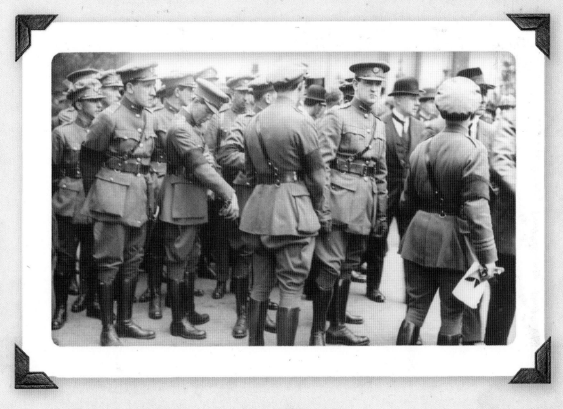

THE IMPERIAL HOTEL, CORK

Michael returned to Cork, to continue his inspection tour and stayed at the Imperial Hotel. Emmet Dalton, who was in charge of the troops in that area, had commandeered the hotel for his HQ as the nearby army barracks had been torched by the anti-Treatyites a few days before.

SLIEVENAMON ARMOURED CAR

Slievenamon, a Rolls Royce Whippet armoured car, originally attached to the British army during the First World War, accompanied Michael and his entourage, on his tour down to West Cork.

**MICHAEL'S FIELD DIARY**
Field diary that Michael kept
with him during his tour to
West Cork. Note the final entry
dated 21/8/22: 'It would be a
big thing to get Civic Guards
both here and in LIMERICK.
Civil Administration urgent
everywhere in the South. The
people are splendid ...'

**THE ELDON HOTEL, SKIBBEREEN**
On Tuesday 22 August, Michael and his party travelled as far as Skibbereen
in West Cork and paid a visit to the proprietors of the Eldon Hotel, the
Quinns. Mrs Teddy Quinn was a daughter of Mrs O'Donovan of 16 Airfield Rd,
Dublin, one of Michael's main 'safe houses' during the War of Independence.
He had become well acquainted with the family during that time.

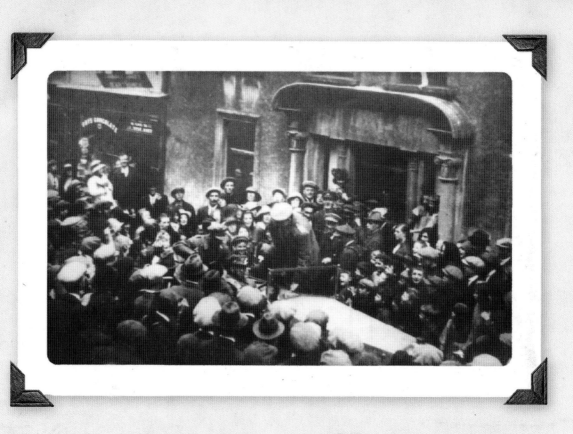

Michael leaving the Eldon Hotel, surrounded by a warm welcoming crowd.

LEES HOTEL, LATER THE MUNSTER ARMS, BANDON
On their return journey to Cork city, Michael and his entourage stopped at
Lees Hotel for tea and another meeting with local pro-Treaty supporters.

Emmet Dalton studies a map beside Michael in the back of their touring car as it roars away from Lees Hotel. It was approaching 8 o'clock in the evening and getting dark. The convoy would shortly enter Béal na mBláth.

# Michael Collins: A life: 1890–1922

Michael Collins was one of the most charismatic figures to emerge from Ireland's struggle for independence in the early part of the twentieth century.

The son of a farmer in remote West Cork, Michael was still only fifteen when he left Ireland to join his sister Hannie in London, the capital city of the British Empire, of which Ireland was still a part. Here, he was to progress from Post Office boy clerk to working as an accountant in a prestigious American bank in the city, work that gave him experience in both financial and organisational skills, which he would put to good use on his return to Dublin in 1916.

Having already been involved with Sinn Féin, the Irish Volunteers and the IRB in London, he quickly rose to prominence following the Easter Rising, when he returned to Ireland after his release from prison in England, in December 1916.

In February 1917 he became secretary of the National Aid Fund and later the same year Director of Organisation. After the setting up of the first Dáil in January 1919, he was initially Minister for Home Affairs but by April became Minister for Finance.

From 1919 to 1921 during the War of Independence, it was his amazing organisational skills and his capacity to understand the minds of the English, with whom he had worked for ten years, that finally brought about a truce between England and Ireland in July 1921.

De Valera initially went over to London to discuss the setting up of an independent Irish republic but soon realised that this was an impossibility with the British government. In October of 1921, a second delegation, headed by Michael, returned to London, but after two months of discussions, which ended with an ultimatum by Lloyd George to sign the Treaty or the war would resume, Michael and his colleagues reluctantly agreed to sign. This led to the setting up of an Irish Free State, excluding the six counties in the North.

In January 1922, Michael was elected Chairman of the Provisional Government of the new Free State and was to spend the next seven months overseeing the departure of British troops and setting up the new Free State's various departments including a new police force and army. However, by July, the Civil War erupted between pro- and anti-Treaty factions and Michael became Commander-in-Chief of his new Free State army. He was also one of its first victims a few weeks later, when his convoy was ambushed and he was shot dead in Béal na mBláth, West Cork on Tuesday 22 August 1922.

So ended his short but amazing life at the age of thirty-one.

# Acknowledgments

I am greatly indebted to the many people who have helped me put together this photograph album on the life of Michael Collins, especially Peter Barry, without whose help this book would not have been published. Also the Collins family, especially Tom Collins of Castlebar, Co. Mayo and Michael Griffin of the Michael Collins Association, Comdt Victor Laing and his colleagues at the Military Archives, Cathal Brugha Barracks, Dublin and Brig. Gen. Ralph James and Michael Whelan at the Irish Air Corps HQ Baldonnel, Dublin, Capt. Dan Harvey of Collins Barracks, Cork and McKee Barracks, Dublin, the Derham, Dicker and O'Donovan families, Isold Ní Dheirg, daughter of Sinead Mason, Melissa Llewelyn Davies, grand-daughter of Moya, the families of Seán MacEoin and Kitty Kiernan.

All the staff of Conns Cameras, Dublin, especially Michael and Bobby, the staff of Reads of Nassau St, Dublin, Sgt Pat McGee, staff at the Garda Museum, Niamh O'Sullivan and the staff at Kilmainham Jail, the staff of Clonakilty and Cork Municipal Museums, Dr Pat Wallace and the National Museum of Ireland, all the staff at the GAA museum at Croke Park, the brothers at the Allen Library, the Frost Collection, the Michael Collins 1922 Society, the staff of the Office of Public Works, the staff of *The Irish Times*, *Irish Independent*, *Examiner*, *The Kerryman* and *Independent* newspapers for their help in researching their photographic archive departments, the staff at Pearse St Library, Dublin and the many people who kindly allowed me to take both exterior and interior photographs of their homes and offices that had been used by Michael, the 1916–21 Club, for allowing me to photograph an original Proclamation owned by themselves.

To Meda Ryan, fellow writer and historian, also Paddy Reidy and Cyril Wall. To my friends Katie Drake who initiated the idea of an album concept for the book and Veronique Crombe for her invaluable photographic and archival assistance. Also to the many people who have helped me compile this book over the last seven years, especially my husband for all his help and support, thank you.